Table of Contents

About the Author

Simone St. Fort is a wife of 36-years and a mother of one. She is presently the full-time pastor at the Deniere Riviere Joyful Assembly, St. Lucia. She was born and raised in the church community. Her ministry involves teaching, preaching, and counseling; especially on issues related to marriage and family.

She holds a Master's Degree in Theology and Counseling, a Bachelor's min Education (U.W.I.) and a Master's Degree in Educational Administration (Leicester University). She is also almost finished completing a Doctorate in Divinity of Counseling. She served as a teacher for twenty-eight (28) years and a principal for sixteen (16); retiring from her full-time job in 2017. She is also the founder and president of the "Hope for Marriages" ministry. She offers counsel and hosts workshops and seminars for many married couples and single individuals, nationwide.

Simone St. Fort is also the founder and president of the "Bridge of Hope Community" foundation, which caters to the needs of the marginalized, underprivileged and vulnerable women in society through skills and educational training.

The church has become a place where only 20% of believers are fulfilling the call of God in their lives. Sadly, too many believers don't even know what their call is! In 2016 the Lord gave me a vision of the urgency for His people to be engaged in Kingdom building. He gave me the theme *Servanthood* as we are called to serve the Kingdom with our all. This book draws on biblical examples to help motivate believers to discover their God-given call and for those who have discovered it, to follow it to completion.

Like Jesus, we were all brought into the Kingdom to serve and not to be served. As a member of the Body of Christ, we must thus function as the part we were created to be. As a non-functional body part affects our entire body, members who are not functioning are hindering the entire Body of Christ from going forward. No one else can do what you were saved to do! At the end of your life, you will be asked to give an account to God, so it is my desire that we all work together until He returns. Do not be found guilty of impeding the Body when you stand before your Master!

INTRODUCTION

God is still waiting for each of us to answer the call. The question God asked Isaiah is still relevant today as it was in old time. "Who shall I send? Who shall go for us?" (Isaiah 6:8). Isaiah responded positively and immediately.

This workbook has been written to assist you the reader in finding your God-given gifts; so, you may help the body of Christ. The intent of this workbook is to be a resource of background information from the book "Servanthood" written by the same author. In it you will find Scripture based questions and lined spaces to write the answers to each question.

Jesus said In Matthew 6:37, "The harvest is plentiful, but the labourers are few." The labourers are few because only a few labourers are working. The world is decayed, and Evil Works are being done more openly now. Secret societies are recruiting members by the hundreds every day. The church is sleeping. Too much energy is spent on non-essential matters in the church. And a few select individuals are used in the services, just to make us feel good and the routine continues.

God is waiting to use each one of us in his service. Once you are able to see what God can do through his most ordinary servants, you will want to answer, 'The Call'. Do not underestimate God's power to work through you to accomplish his will on earth. Are you feeling inadequate, ungifted, fearful, timid or overextended? As you go through the book Servanthood and its supplemental workbook, you will see how God settles these issues.

The Apostle Peter was unlearned and vulgar just like any fisherman. God used him tremendously! Together with John they healed a cripple man (Acts 3:1-10). Ananias and Sapphira were pronounced dead immediately after Peter discerned that they had lied to the Holy Spirit (Acts 5:1-

10). The shadow of Peter healed the sick as they laid them on beds and mats on the street (Acts 5:15-16). God mightily used Paul, who persecuted the early church; even handkerchiefs and aprons that touched him were taken to the sick and their illnesses were cured, and evil spirits left them (Acts 19:11-12).

What are you doing with the call of God on your life? Are you a labourer? Well start to work. The task is great. Get involved. Paul started doing God's work just as he got saved.

May God bless you as you endeavour to search the scriptures which will motivate you to answer the call or find your calling in the Master's vineyard. The wisest man that ever-lived writes, "All hard work brings a profit, but mere talk leads only to poverty." So just do it

Chapter 1
The Concept of Servanthood

1. The word servant usually brings a negative feeling to many people even in the Body of Christ. However, from the Old Testament through the New Testament, God has used the term "servant" to refer to his people. Look back at the following scriptures and identify who is spoken of as a servant.

   a. Genesis 26:24

____

   b. Exodus 14:31

____

   c. Numbers 14:24

____

   d. 1 Samuel 3:9

____

   e. Psalms 89:3

____

2. There is a thin line between a "slave" and a "servant".
Give the distinction between the two terms.

____

____

____

____

____

3. According to Romans 6:16-18 two types of slaves are
mentioned. List and explain each one.

____

____

____

____

____

4. How does God view Christians as servants in the early realm? (Refer to Ephesians 6:6)

____

____

____

____

____

5. The apostle Paul so loved the idea of a servant that he wanted men to regard the followers of Christ as servants, servants in this regard means "home manager" or "steward" (1 Corinthians: 4:11). According to 1 Corinthians 2:7, what privilege do Christians have as servants of God?

____

____

____

____

6. In today's world we often find that those in lesser circumstances are in a position of serving those who are more affluent. Matthew 23:11 establishes a biblical perspective which is somewhat different. Jesus Christ was a perfect example of servanthood. List at least five (5) humbling circumstances in which he ministered to his followers.

____

____

____

____

____

____

7. In your own words elaborate on true greatness as brought
   out in Matthew 23:11

____

____

____

____

8. In the book of John 13:13-17, Jesus illustrated a beautiful
   lesson of servanthood. He humbled himself to wash his
   disciples' feet. He told his disciples that he as their master
   had to demonstrate his servanthood. What lesson can be
   learned from this illustration?

____

____

____

____

9. Many Christians do not feel comfortable performing menial tasks in working for God. In Matthew 20:26-28 and Luke 22:25-27, Jesus explained the concept of true Servanthood. Identify at least two characteristics of servanthood from the scriptures.

____

____

____

____

10. Jesus found it was an honour to be called a servant of his Father. In John 6:38, He stated that he came not to do his own will but the work of his Father. Again, in John 17:4 Jesus told his Father that he brought him glory on earth by completing the work that he gave him to do.

In what way can you make Jesus Proud of you, his servant?

____

____

____

____

Chapter 2
Know Your Calling

1. A spiritual gift is a special attribute given by the Holy Spirit to <u>every member</u> of the Body of Christ according to God's grace for use within the context of the Body of Christ.

   Expound on the underlined phrase.

   ____

   ____

   ____

   ____

   ____

   ____

   ____

2. Paul noted in 1 Corinthians 12:1, "Now about spiritual gifts, brothers, I don't want you to be ignorant."

Explain a possible reason why you think Paul made that statement.

____

____

____

____

____

____

3. According to 1 Corinthians 12:8-10 Paul listed a number of gifts given by the Holy Spirit. Identify each one of them.

____

____

____

____

4. To better understand the gifts mentioned above and their function and operations they can be classified into three categories. Each category has three gifts. Use the gifts you identified above and place them into the correct categories.

Gifts of Vocal Inspiration (Speaking)

____

____

____

Revelation Gifts (Hearing)

____

____

____

Power Gifts (Doing)

____

____

____

5. Write your own definition of the Gifts of the Spirit you
listed.

i.
____

____

ii.
____

____

iii.
____

____

iv.
____

____

v.
____

____

vi.
____

____

vii.
____

____

viii.
____

____

ix. _______________________________

____

6. In Ephesians 4:11-12 another set of gifts are mentioned.

   List and define them.

   ____

   ____

   ____

   ____

   ____

   ____

   ____

7. Many Christians treat lightly their lack

   operating/functioning in their God given gifts. Paul

   clearly outlined the purpose of the gifts. Study Ephesians

4:12-13 and name at least three reasons why God

distributed gifts to the Body of Christ.

____

____

____

____

____

8. Paul used the physical body to make a comparison to the

spiritual body of Jesus Christ. Outline the main

comparison (1 Corinthians 12:12-31)

____

____

____

____

____

9. Paul was very concerned that the gifts were not dormant.
He admonished young Timothy in 2 Timothy 1:6,
"Therefore I remind you to stir up the gift of God which is
in you through the laying on of my hands."
What do you think the phrase, 'stir up the gift of God
mean?'

____

____

____

____

____

10. Do you think one can stifle the Body of Christ? Explain
how. (Refer to Ephesians 4:13-14)

____

____

____

____

11. The Apostle Paul in Romans 12:6-8 spoke about getting another set of spiritual gifts. Using your first list of gifts compare it to those gifts being mentioned and write any new ones you have not listed.

____

____

____

12. Jesus Christ did not only minister to people's physical needs when he was on earth. Nor does he expect us to only see about people's physical needs.

Do you think our gifts as Christians are only to minister to the spiritual needs of people like preaching and teaching?

(Read Matthew 25:35-40)

____

____

____

____

13. How does Christ expect us to minister to other needs? List

at least three different ways that we can minister to

people's needs according to Matthew 25:35-40)

i. _______________________________________

____

ii. _______________________________________

____

iii. _______________________________________

____

14. Identify three ways in which you can minister to people

outside of the church.

i. _______________________________________

____

ii. _______________________________________

____

iii. _______________________________________

____

15. The Bible clearly states that good works cannot save us
from sin Ephesians 2:8-9. However, when we become
Christians, we must do good works.

There are people in the bible that performed good deeds.

a) In 2 Kings 4:8-36, the Bible speaks of a woman of
God who was hospitable.

Identify who this woman was and the act of kindness
she performed.

____

____

____

____

What was her reward?

____

____

____

b) Read Acts 9:36-41.

Identify the person and say what works she

performed.

____

____

____

What was her reward?

____

____

____

16. The Bible admonished us in Hebrews 13:2 read and

explain the term, "don't forget to entertain strangers."

____

____

____

____

____

17. A secular job can be compared to that of a Christian work in many ways. A good job with great pay, good co-workers and good benefits. However, it demands great commitment. A lot of work goes undone without commitment. It is said by researchers that only ten percent of workers do the majority of the work. Many Christians are in the same boat. They are saved but not doing much for God.

a) Why is this? Give five possible answers

    i.   ________________________________

    ii. ________________________________

    iii. ________________________________

    iv. ________________________________

    v.   ________________________________

b) What can be done about it?

____

____

____

____

____

c) Many things may hinder the call of God upon your

life. Sometimes you may not answer the call. List

some reasons God speaks to his people in doing his

work.

____

____

____

____

____

18. a) Do you remember when God called you to do his

work? _______________________________________

c) How did you respond?

____

____

19. Write down Romans 11:29, what lesson did you learn

from it?

Romans 11:29

____

____

____

____

____

____

20. The basis for all Christian service is found in Mark 16:15

but many Christians believe that spreading the gospel is

the duty of only some Christians. According to the

scripture, what do you think?

____

____

____

____

____

21. List at least ten ways you can actively participate in the
Lords work and in so doing help to fulfil the great
commission.

i. ____

____

ii. ____

____

iii. ____

____

iv. ____

____

v. ____

____

vi. ____

____

vii. ____

____

viii. _______________________________

____

ix. _______________________________

____

x. _______________________________

____

22. Look back at the list you create above and put a tick next to the activities that you may be engaged in and that the church may not see or know that you are doing.

23. a) The devil always attempts to delude Christians into thinking that we were placed on earth just to live and die. Read Isaiah 43:7 and Ephesians 2:10 what do you learn from these verses.

____

____

____

b) Do your daily decisions reflect this determination?

Explain your answer.

24. The windows of travel agencies are filled with posters

meant to lure us to faraway places. If you stepped inside

the agent would unfold colourful brochures and talk at

length of the wonderful adventures of travel. But of

course, there is a price to pay.

The service of God is exciting. But there is a price to pay

if we are willing to follow this way also.

What do you think "paying the price" means with respect to God's service?

____

____

____

____

____

25. How does Romans 12:1 bear on this subject.

____

____

____

26. There are some principles established in scripture concerning the call of God. (1Corintians 9:16-17). What points do you find in these verses?

27. a) Willing service to God should be more an attitude than

obligation. Psalms 40:8 contains a key word which

reflects a certain attitude that we should maintain as we

serve the Lord. Note the word and describe how you think

it applies to our Christian service.

b) Now briefly describe how an opposite attitude might affect our service.

____

____

____

____

____

28. Isaiah heard the voice of the Lord saying, "whom shall I send? And who will go for me?" You may not be able to go oversees to fulfil the call of God but there are several ways you can. Write at least three ways you can heed the call of God in your personal life.

____

____

____

____

____

Notes:

Chapter 3
God of Excellent and Extraordinary

1. Isaiah 55:8 declares, "for my thought are not your thoughts neither are your ways my ways, declares the Lord."

   What do you think God is teaching us in this verse?

   ____

   ____

   ____

   ____

   ____

In the Bible we realize that God used extra ordinary things and people to minister his will.

2. Read Joshua 10:12-13

   a. Which heavenly element did he allow to go beyond nature?

      ____

      ____

      ____

      ____

b. What did he want Joshua his servant to accomplish?

____

____

____

____

____

3. Read 2 Kings 20:9-10

   a. What was the abnormal circumstance used in the scripture verses?

____

____

____

____

____

   b. What did he accomplish?

____

____

____

____

____

4. Read Numbers 22:27-30

    a. What creature did he use?

    ____

    ____

    ____

    ____

    ____

    b. What were the three circumstances surrounding
        this event?

    ____

    ____

    ____

    ____

    ____

5. What can be deduced from the three circumstances
    above?

    ____

    ____

    ____

    ____

    ____

6. The devil usually brings back our past lives to keep us away from doing God's work. With God on our side, the past does not define our qualifications to be accepted as a worker for God.

Have you felt at any time that you don't deserve the calling of God?

____

____

____

____

____

7. 1 Corinthians 1:26-29 state," Brothers, think of what you were when you were called. Not many of you were wise by human standards; not many were influential; not many were of noble birth. But God chose the foolish things of the world to shame the wise; God chose the weak things of the world to shame the strong. He chose the lowly things of the world and despised things and the things that are not to nullify the things that are, so that no one may boast before him."

Conduct a self-assessment and tick the category you fell in before you got saved.

___ wise

___ influential

___ noble

___ foolish

___ weak

___lowly

___ despised

8. You are qualified. How does the phrase "Therefore there is now no condemnation for those who are in Christ Jesus…." Romans 8:1; relate to the above scripture in 1 Corinthians 1:26-29.

____

____

____

____

____

The Bible has countless examples of men and women who were counted as nobodies in the eyes of men, but God used them mightily to perform great acts. For too long Christians have underestimated God's desire to work through them to accomplish his work.

Let's examine the Bible verses below:

9. Exodus 2:11-14

    a. Who is the text talking about?

____

    b. What crime did he commit?

____

Exodus 4:10-14

    c. What was his excuse?

____

Exodus 6:30

    d. What was his second excuse?

____

Exodus 7:10

    e. How old was he when God called him?

____

We see that yes; he was a murderer who stammered but became eloquent and powerful after encountering God.

10. 1 Samuel 16:11-14

    a. This young lad was selected by God above his brothers. Who was he?

____

    b. What was his occupation at the time?

____

2 Samuel 11:2-5

    c.   What sin was committed?

____

2 Samuel 11:14

    d.   What other sin was committed?

____

The young shepherd boy became an adulterer and later a murderer but after confessing and forsaking his mistakes, God continued to use him mightily.

11. Joshua 2:1-4

    a.   What was the event taking place?

____

____

____

    b.   Who did God use to save his people?

____

____

12. According to James 2:25, how did God perceive that woman?

____

____

____

____

____

Note in Matthew 1:5, that woman although a prostitute, was mentioned in the genealogy of Jesus Christ. In Hebrews 11:31, her name was written in the hall of fame.

13. Judges 4:4-7

    a. What   was   the   name   of   the   woman?

       ____

    b. Name   the   two   positions   she   had?

       ____

Judges 4:9

    c. Why did God give the victory to a woman?

       ____

14. Sometimes God allows his people to go through bad experiences to achieve a purpose.

Genesis 37:2-8

    a. What was the scenario?

       ____

       ____

       ____

       ____

Genesis 39:19

    b. What misfortune happened to Joseph?

____

____

____

Genesis 41:41

    c. What was Joseph's reward?

____

____

____

Genesis 45:4-5

    d. What was God's purpose for Joseph?

____

____

____

15. John 4:7-42

How did this prostitute affect the kingdom of darkness after meeting Jesus?

____

____

____

____

____

16. Who were some characters extraordinarily used in the Bible? Think of Abraham, Peter, Esther, Ruth, Paul and describe what kind of person each was and what greatness followed them?

____

____

____

____

____

____

____

____

____

Chapter 4
Spiritual Power: Vital for Effective Service

1. In the Book of Zachariah 4:6 states, "so he said to me, this is the word of the Lord" to Zerubbabel: not by my might nor by power, but by my spirit, says the Lord Almighty. Study the text and attempt to define

   a. Might

   ____

   ____

   ____

   b. Power_________________________________

   ____

   ____

   c. Why do you think Zerubbabel's own effort could not complete the building of the temple?

   ____

   ____

   ____

   ____

   ____

2. We can clearly see the role of the Holy Spirit from creation through present times. The Holy Spirit has always empowered God's people to do extraordinary work. Study the following scriptures in the Old Testament where the spirit of God moved upon these people because the Holy Spirit was not poured in full as yet.

a.   Read Judges 3:10

  i.   Who was the man of God?

  ____

  ii.   Why did the Spirit of God come upon him?

  ____

  ____

  iii.   What was his victory?

  ____

b.   Read Judges 11:29

  i.   Name the person from the text.

  ____

  ii.   Why did he need the power of the Holy Spirit?

  ____

  ____

  ____

  iii.   What was his victory?

  ____

  ____

c. Read Judges 14:6-9

    i. Name the person in the text.

    ____

    ii. Why did the spirit of God come upon him?

    ____

    ____

d. Read 1 Samuel 16:6-13

    i. Name the young man?

    ____

    ii. Why was he anointed?

    ____

    ____

    ____

e. Read 1 Samuel 10:9-12

    i. Who is the text talking about?

    ____

    ii. Why was he anointed?

    ____

    ____

    ____

3. In the New Testament, the Holy Spirit was poured out in full as was prophesied in

Joel 2:28-29. "I will pour out my Spirit on all people, your sons and daughters will prophesy, your old men will dream dreams, your young men will see visions. Even on my servants, both men and women, I will pour out my spirit in those days."

According to the text, do you think that the outpouring of the Spirit is for you? _________

Give   a   reason(s)   for   your   answer.

____

____

____

____

____

4. There was no miracle recorded during the first thirty years in Jesus' life.

After he was baptised by John the Baptist, according to Mark 1:10-11, then the Holy Spirit came upon Him. Immediately miracles began to happen in his ministry.

a. In what form did the Holy Spirit appear upon Jesus?

____

____

____

b. Why do you think this experience was so important to Jesus?

____

____

c. List at least five miracles Jesus performed after his baptism.

   i. _______________________________

   ii. _______________________________

   iii. _______________________________

   iv. _______________________________

   v. _______________________________

5. After the baptism of Jesus, he quoted an Old Testament prophecy from Isaiah 61:1-3 in Luke 4:18-19.

   a. What was Jesus' assignment after receiving the baptism of the Holy Spirit?

   ____

   ____

   ____

   ____

   b. Do you think that you have these same assignments?

   ____

   ____

   Why?

   ____

   ____

6. Read Acts 6:3

The Apostle thought it would be too much work for them to do everything. Consequently, they asked the people to choose men to serve food and so on.

a. Write two qualifications that were required of the seven deacons:

____

____

____

____

b. Why do you think the deacons should be filled with the Holy Spirit to serve natural things?

____

____

____

____

7. One may tend to believe that only the Jews received the baptism of the Holy Spirit.

a. Read Acts 8 14 -17

i.   Name the group that received?

____

____

ii.   How did the experience happen?

____

____

b. Read Acts 10:44-46

iii.   Name the group that received?

____

____

iv.   How did the experience happen?

____

____

c. Read Acts 19:2-6

v.   Name the group that received?

____

____

vi.   How did the experience happen?

____

____

8. Acts 1:4-5, the apostles were asked to tarry. Why?

____

____

____

____

9. No matter how talented, smart or educated you are, you
need the baptism of the Holy Spirit. Jesus was specific
when he asked the disciples to wait in Acts 1:8.
What was promised to them?

____

____

____

____

____

10. This tarrying would enable them to be more effective
witnesses for God because of the boldness and power.

a. Name the places they were to witness for Christ?

____

____

____

____

____

b. How can you witness for Christ?

____

____

____

____

____

11. The Apostle Peter received that boldness in Acts 2:1-4, 36-41.

    a. How many people were saved?

    ____

    ____

    ____

    b. Do you think God still desires such results?

    ____

    Why?

    ____

    ____

    ____

    ____

    ____

12. Peter heals a cripple man in Acts 3:1-10. How did Peter make it clear that the power of healing did not come from him (verse 6)?

____

____

____

____

____

13. When we talk about power for service, we may think in the line of preaching, teaching etc. but God wants us to have the power even in serving tables. This means no matter what, we all need that power from on high.

   a. Have you been baptised with the Holy Ghost?

____

Why?

____

____

   b. Whose responsibility is it to be filled with the Holy Spirit?

____

____

____

14. Do you think the baptism of the Hold Spirit is for you today (Acts 2:36-42)?

____

____

____

15. Can you be an effective worker for God without being empowered by the Holy Spirit?

(1 Corinthians 2:3-4 and 2 Corinthians 3:5-6)

Chapter 5
Consequences and Rewards

Jesus was educating his disciples regarding his departure, their responsibility after he went away and his eventual return. He used similar parables in Luke 19:12-17 and Matthew 25:14-30.

1. In Luke 19:12-17, the story spoke about a nobleman. The word nobleman means 'person of noble blood, usually princely'.

    Give evidence as to whom you think the nobleman represents in this parable (see Hebrews 12:2)

    ____

    ____

    ____

2. The word servant means "slave bondman or servant of a King". It also means one who gives himself up wholly to another's will or dominion.

    Who do you think the servants represent?

    ____

    ____

    ____

    ____

3. In Matthew 25, each servant was given a talent; 75 lbs. List various gifts or talents which you think the talent may represent.

____

____

____

____

____

4. The nobleman called his servants to determine how much each man had gained by trading. How did the first two servants differ from the third one?

____

____

____

____

5. The last servant never traded his pounds. Identify this error and interpret its meaning.

____

____

____

____

____

6. The two servants who traded were called faithful.
    Consider and note several actions which we could take
    to ensure a reward in eternity as faithful stewards.

____

____

____

____

7. Who is a steward of the Lord?

____

____

____

____

8. What is the reward of being found faithful in your
    stewardship?

____

____

____

____

9. Do you feel it is equally important for us today to use what God has given us, as it was for the servants in the lesson?

____

Explain your answer?

____

____

____

____

10. The nobleman gave the ten talents according to abilities. He was looking for interest. Describe some of the gains one can experience in working for the Lord.

____

____

____

____

11. Paraphrase the nobleman's statement to his servants. "occupy till I come":

____

____

____

____

12. Those who seek spiritual gain in the gospel for themselves and others will become richer and those who neglect or squander what is given to them will become poorer.

Are you a good steward?

____

Explain your answer.

____

____

____

____

13. In your own words explain, "To whom much is given, much is required." Luke 12:48:

____

____

____

____

14. Do you think the lesson of being a good steward applies to the way we work in school or on the job?

____

____

Explain why.

____

____

____

____

____

____

15. How does God feel towards those who labour for Him?
Refer to Hebrews 6:10.

____

____

____

16. 1 Corinthians 15:58 (NIV) states, "Therefore, my dear
brothers and sisters, stand firm. Let nothing move you.
Always give yourselves fully to the work of the Lord,
because you know that your labour in the Lord is not in
vain".
According to the text how can you encourage someone
to labour for the Lord?

____

____

____

____

Appendix

This is a guide to help you identify your spiritual gift.

The Five-Fold Ministry

These five gifts are also known as the Five-Fold Ministry. They are also referred to as the Ascension gifts because they were released to earth when Jesus ascended to heaven (Ephesians 4:9-11). They are Apostles, Prophet, Evangelists, Teachers and Pastors.

See if you have the attributes of the Five-Fold Ministry	Yes	No
ARE YOU CALLED TO BE AN APOSTLE? *Do you mobilize gifts? Do you impart calling or gift?* *Do you have a deep concern for unity in the Body of Christ?* *Do you lay foundations for new congregations?* *Do you keep Christians founded on Christ?* If yes, then you are called to be an Apostle.		

ARE YOU CALLED TO BE A PROPHET? *Do you thrust believers forward in their vision?* *Do you articulate spiritual gifts?* *Do you call believers to holiness and righteousness?* *Do you impart a spirit of prayer and intersession?* *Do you have a heart to edify, comfort and exhort?* *Do you lay foundations upon Christ in individuals and ministries?* *Do you speak words with creative power to change?* If yes, then you have a Prophet's gift.		
ARE YOU CALLED TO BE AN EVANGALIST? *Do you bring the conviction of Christ to individuals and crowds to the point where people feel compelled by God?* *Do you stir up the body of Christ to reach the lost, to have a burden for evangelism?* *Do you bring conviction of sin?* *Do you help people to receive Christ and become established in local congregation?* *Do you stir people to action to respond to God?*		

Do you cause unbelievers to find salvation and forgiveness? *Do you break bondages of excuses, inactivity, laziness and indecisiveness?* *Do you help people to understand and respond to the basic biblical message of salvation, cleansing, baptism ant the gifts of the spirit?* *Do you disciple other Evangelist and release them into the Body of Christ?* If yes, then you are an evangelist.		
ARE YOU CALLED TO BE A TEACHER? *Are you particular about accuracy in handling God's word?* *Do you enable believers to understand God's truth?* *Do you set believers free from deception and error?* *Do you unfold a practical lifestyle that fits with sound doctrine?* *Do you help people to live by principles and not circumstances?* If yes, you have a teacher's gift.		

ARE YOU CALLED TO BE A PASTOR?

Do you speak in a way that brings security and acceptance?

Can you draw people together in Christ, gathering them into the body?

Do you feel for people, concerned about their point of view?

Are you intimately involved with your congregation, small groups?

Do you lead and feed people what is good for growth?

Do you break bondages of independence, isolation and insecurity?

Do you offer counsel and love to people?

If yes, you have a Pastors' gift.

There are also other gifts given to the Body of Christ. Continue reading to find out where you are called.

	DESCRIPTION	SCRIPTURE
SERVICE	The gift of service is the special ability that God gives to certain members of the Body of Christ to identify the unmet needs involved in a task related to God's work, and to accomplish the desired goals.	Romans 12:7 Ephesians 6:5-9
INTERCESSION	The gift of intercession is the special ability that God gives to certain members of the Body of Christ to pray for extended periods of time on a regular basis and see frequent and specific answers to their prayers to a degree much greater than that which is expected of the average Christian.	1 Timothy 2:1-2 Colossians 6:5-9
HOSPITALITY	The gift of Hospitality is the special ability that God gives to certain members of the Body of Christ to provide an open house and warm welcome to those in need of food and lodging.	Acts 16: 15 Romans 12:9-13 Hebrews 13:1-2 1 Peter 4:9

LEADERSHIP	The gift of leadership is the special ability that God gives to certain members of the Body of Christ to set goals in accordance with God's purpose for the future and to communicate those goals to others in such a way that they voluntarily and harmoniously work together to accomplish those goals for the glory of God.	
FAITH		Acts 11:22-24, Acts 27:21-25 1 Corinthians 12:9
ADMINISTRATION	The gift of administration is the special ability that God gives to certain members of the Body of Christ to understand clearly immediate and long-range goals of a particular unit of the Body of Christ and to devise and execute effective plans for the accomplishment of those goals.	Acts 6:1-7 1 Corinthians 12:9
MISSIONARY	The gift of missionary is the special ability that God gives to certain members of the Body of Christ to minister their unique spiritual gifts in a second culture.	Acts 8:4-5,1 3:2-3, 22:21 1 Corinthians 9:19-23 Ephesians 3:7-8

WISDOM	The gift of wisdom is the special ability that God gives to certain members of the Body of Christ to know the mind of the Holy Spirit and receive insight into how given knowledge may best be applied to specific needs arising in the Body of Christ.	Acts 6:3, 10 1 Corinthians 12:8 James 1:5-6 2 Peter 3:15
HELPS	The gift of helps is the special ability that God gives to certain members of the Body of Christ to invest the talents they have in the life and ministry of other members of the Body, thus enabling the person to increase the effectiveness of his or her spiritual gifts.	Romans 16:1-2 1 Corinthians 12:28
GIVING	The gift of giving is the special ability that God gives to certain members of the Body of Christ to contribute their material resources to the work of the Lord with Liberality and cheerfulness.	Matthew 26:6-8 Acts 4: 32 – 37
DISCERNMENT	The gift of discernment is the special ability that God gives to certain members of the Body of Christ to know with assurance whether certain behaviour purported to be of God is in reality divine, human or satanic.	Acts 16:16-18 1 Corinthians 12:10 1 John 4:1-6

EXHORTATION	The gift of exhortation is the special ability that God gives to certain members of the Body of Christ to minister words of comfort, consolation, encouragement and counsel to other members of the Body in such a way that they feel helped and healed.	Acts 14:22 Romans 12:8 1 Timothy 4:13 Hebrew 10:25
SINGER		1 Corinthians 12:8

TEACHER OF SONG	To teach others to sing the Songs of the Lord. To instruct the congregation to sing and to play their instrument in harmony unto the Lord. To lead the church choir. To be an instructor in voice.	
MUSICIAN	To play an instrument skilfully unto the Lord through music. To inspire others to play or sing unto the Lord. To edify the people of God through music. To be a skilful member of the church orchestra.	
DOORKEEPER	To warmly greet visitors arriving at a church. To help people find seats in the church as an usher. To serve the congregation at church in similar and practical ways.